BRAIN BOOSTERS

NATURE PUZZLES

by
Vicky Barker
& Ste Johnson

LiTtle GENIUS BOOks

Published by Little Genius Books. www.littlegeniusbooks.com. • 10 9 8 7 6 5 4 3 2 1 • 9781953344434

Add sad faces or happy faces to these fish.
Draw their scales and color them in.

Follow the turtle's path to find out where it is heading.

_____

3

Carl eats only leaves with even answers.
Carly eats only the ones with odd answers.
Which caterpillar eats the most leaves?

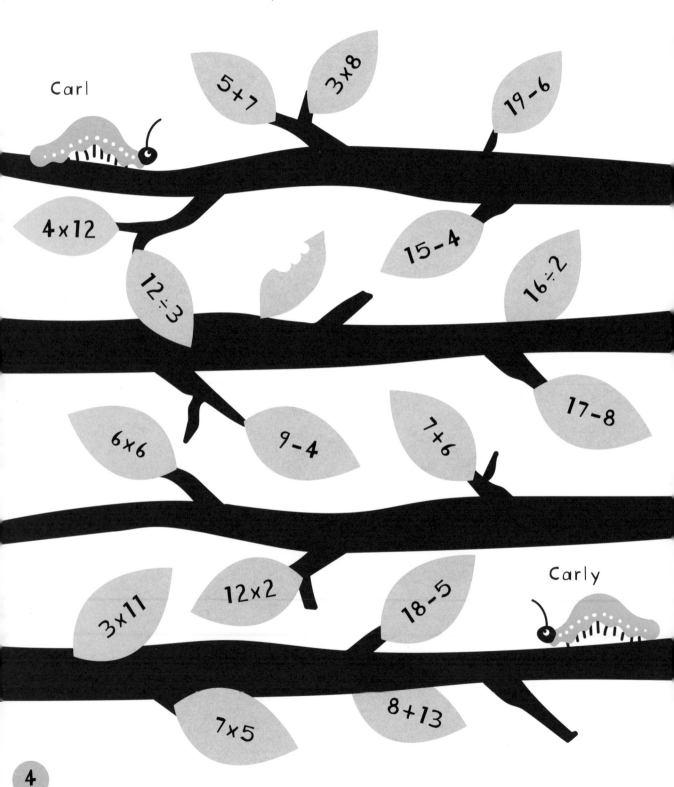

Carl

5+7

3×8

19-6

4×12

15-4

12÷3

16÷2

6×6

9-4

7+6

17-8

Carly

3×11

12×2

18-5

7×5

8+13

Finish these patterns found in nature.
Can you think of any more?

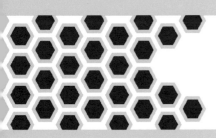

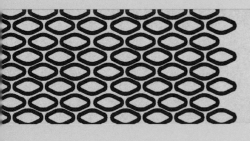

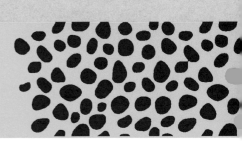

DID YOU KNOW? Camouflage can help animals to hide from predators or to hunt for prey.

Connect the dots to add some fishy friends to this coral reef. Color in the beautiful scene.

Add symmetrical patterns to the shells
of these baby sea turtles.

DID YOU KNOW?

Leatherback sea turtles have been
known to dive over 3,000 feet
(1,000 m) deep in the ocean.

Help this bee
get to the flower.

Coral reefs are full of dashing colors and stunning fish.
Create your own colorful scene below.

DID YOU KNOW?

Coral reefs look like
complicated rock structures,
but they are actually made
up of animals called corals
and plants called algae.

Dive into this underwater word search.

F	Y	D	I	V	E	R	S	V	M	S	H	H	S	H	K
I	S	X	K	T	U	R	T	P	E	U	S	X	T	M	T
S	S	Q	S	P	E	C	I	E	S	I	L	U	U	A	R
D	T	O	U	W	R	H	M	K	F	D	H	S	R	X	O
H	A	L	R	I	Q	J	H	A	L	G	A	E	T	M	P
P	R	F	E	V	D	E	B	L	M	A	X	A	L	J	I
L	F	E	F	D	S	L	E	N	H	X	H	W	E	H	C
K	I	E	F	X	L	L	A	R	O	C	E	M	S	A
E	S	R	B	E	G	Y	X	P	O	C	X	E	V	H	L
Y	H	P	H	S	K	F	M	C	R	T	X	D	H	A	M
F	D	S	L	O	W	I	N	K	L	O	U	Q	W	R	A
B	U	B	B	L	E	S	X	D	X	P	V	X	U	K	R
Q	L	G	X	J	F	H	N	X	M	U	K	E	L	P	C
G	R	O	C	E	A	N	S	H	E	S	K	L	E	S	M
J	A	L	S	E	A	W	R	E	F	L	L	E	H	K	P
K	B	A	D	E	E	P	S	E	A	X	M	B	A	R	C

FISH	**OCEAN**	**SHARK**	**JELLYFISH**
CORAL	**OCTOPUS**	**DEEP SEA**	**SEAWEED**
REEF	**DIVER**	**BUBBLES**	**SPECIES**
KELP	**STARFISH**	**ALGAE**	**SQUID**
TROPICAL	**TURTLE**	**SHELL**	**CRAB**

Each of these rows of flowers has a different number pattern. Can you work out the pattern and fill in the blank spaces?

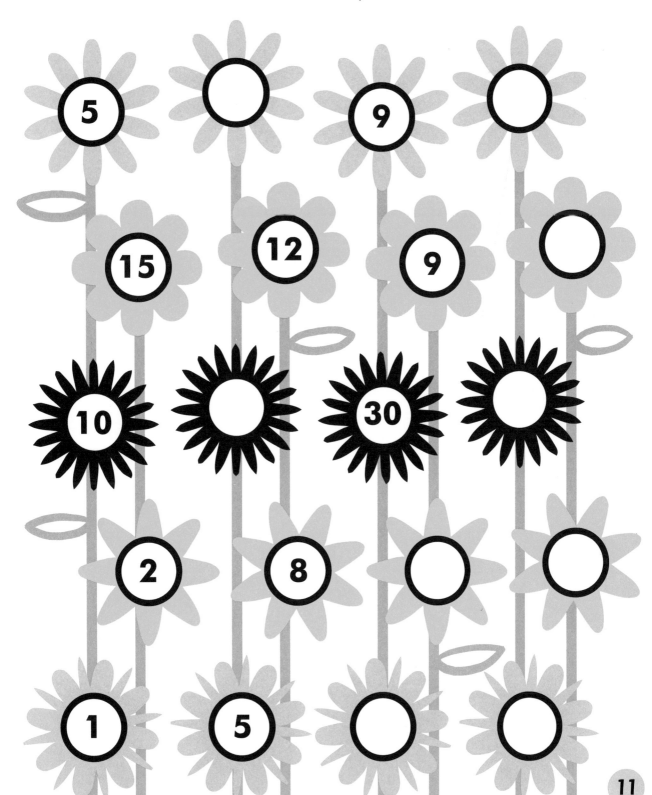

Find the odd one out in each row.

1.

2.

3.

4.

5.

Match these deep-sea creatures to their shadows.

True or false?

1. In Svalbard, Norway, it is light from mid-April to mid-August with no night.

2. If a fish holds its breath long enough, it can float out of the water and start to fly.

3. The Sahara Desert is 3,000 miles (4,800 k) wide.

4. The largest ocean is the Indian Ocean.

5. There are around 12 times more trees on Earth than stars in the Milky Way galaxy.

6. Pineapples take a year to grow.

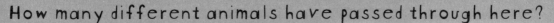

How many different animals have passed through here?

DID YOU KNOW?

Animal tracks can tell you what kind of animal
made them, how large it was, when the tracks were made,
and how fast the animal was traveling at that time.

Can you spot ten differences in these scenes?

DID YOU KNOW? The word cephalopod comes from the Greek word for "head-feet." Common types of cephalopods include octopuses, squid, and cuttlefish.

Help this firefly find its
way back to its friends.

START
HERE

18

Use this step-by-step guide to draw a sleepy sloth.

Find the group of fish that matches the group on the right.

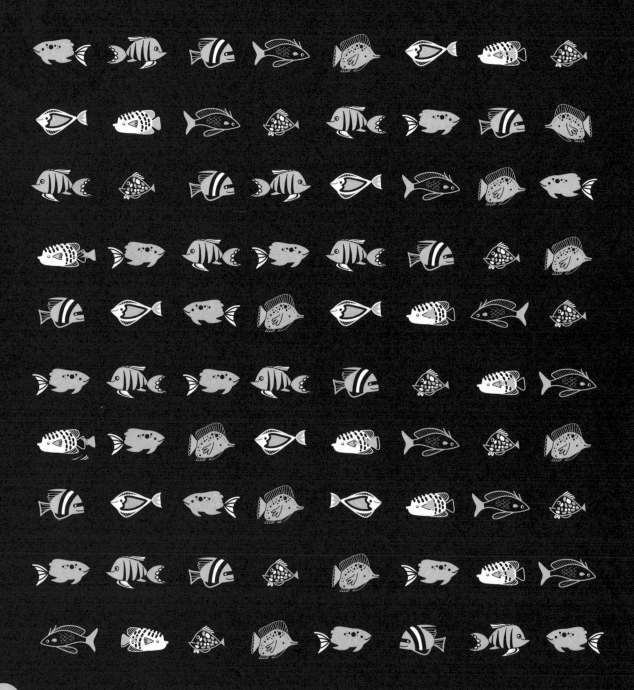

You have discovered a new species
of insect in the depths of the rainforest!
Draw what it looks like and give it a name.

21

Reunite this goat with its friend, and guide them both safely back up the mountain. Watch out for clouds and trees blocking your path.

START HERE

22

Draw the rest of these butterflies and color them in.

DID YOU KNOW?

Butterflies have transparent wings, and they taste with their feet.

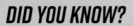

How quickly can you get this baby shark back to its dad?
Draw a line as fast as you can without going off the path.
Time yourself!

Can you copy this toucan picture in the grid below?

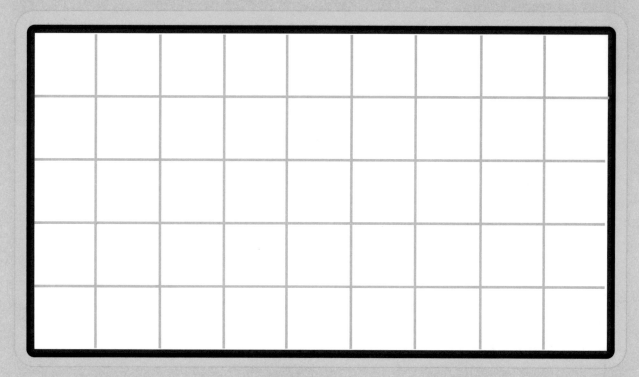

START
HERE

26

Subtract all the spaces with a dot marked in them by coloring them in. You will reveal a picture with the spaces left behind!

Are these bees or ladybugs? You decide!

DID YOU KNOW?

To produce a pound of honey, bees fly the equivalent of three times around the world.

Can you work out the answers to these?

Add patterns to these shells.

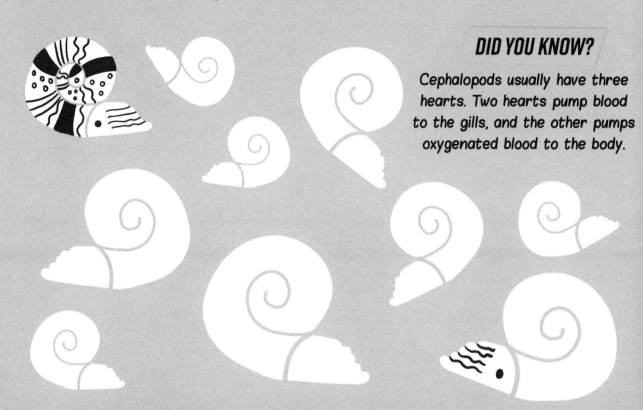

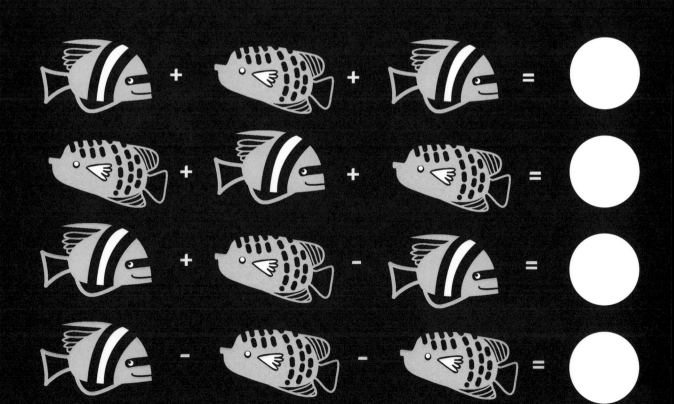

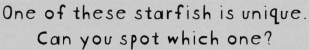

One of these starfish is unique.
Can you spot which one?

DID YOU KNOW?

Starfish have no brain or blood. They use
filtered sea water to pump nutrients
through their nervous system.

Are there more fireflies or stars?

DID YOU KNOW?

Fireflies are not actually flies. They are a type of bioluminescent beetle.

What is out of place in this scene?

Can you work out the sequence that these shells follow?
Fill in the blank shells with the right pattern.

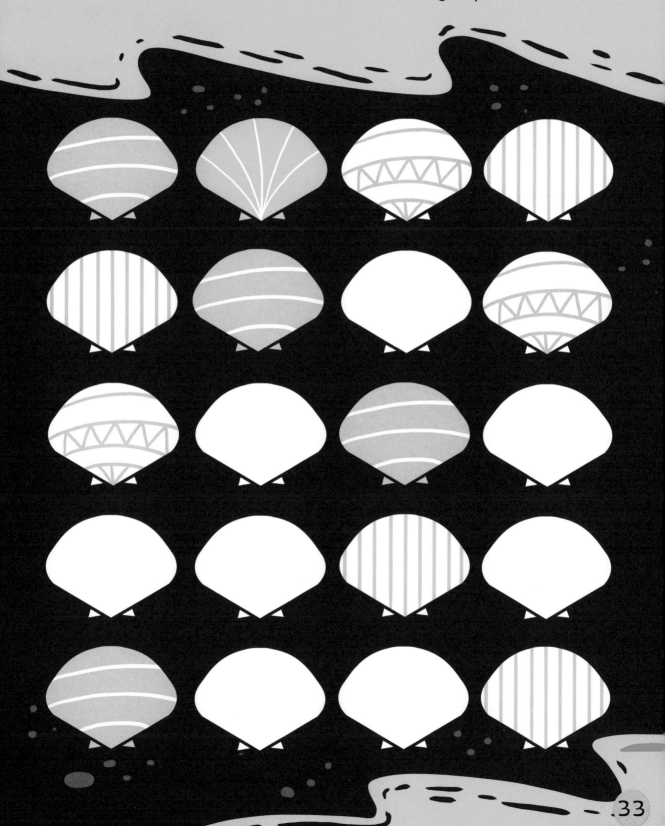

34

Busy beehive word search!
Find all of these words in the grid below.

HIVE
HONEY
QUEEN
COLONY
BUZZ

FLOWER
POLLEN
SWARM
WAX
INSECT

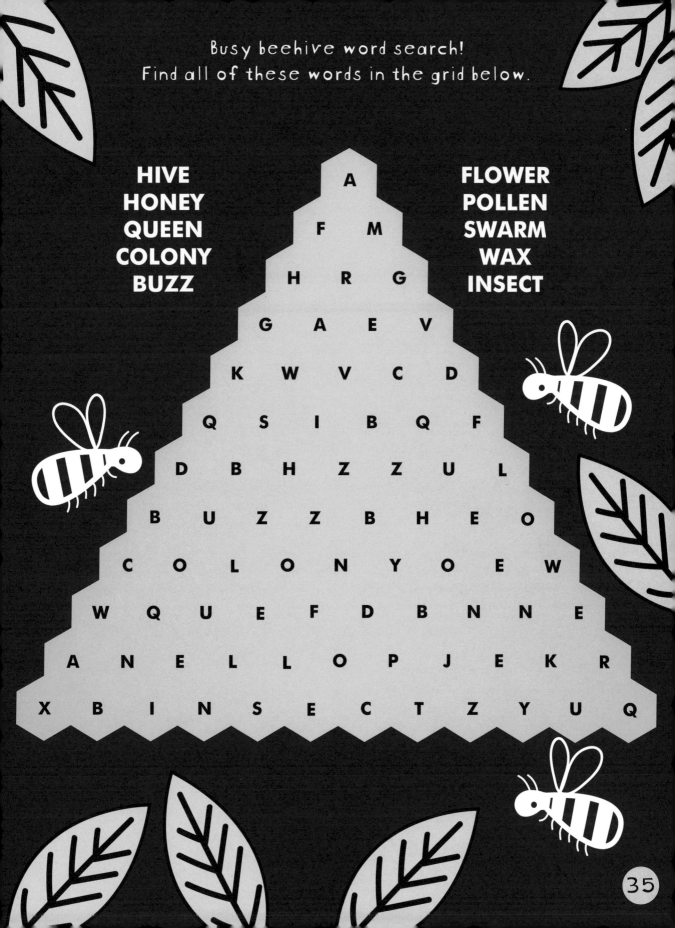

```
            A
          F   M
        H   R   G
      G   A   E   V
    K   W   V   C   D
  Q   S   I   B   Q   F
D   B   H   Z   Z   U   L
B   U   Z   Z   B   H   E   O
C   O   L   O   N   Y   O   E   W
W   Q   U   E   F   D   B   N   N   E
A   N   E   L   L   O   P   J   E   K   R
X   B   I   N   S   E   C   T   Z   Y   U   Q
```

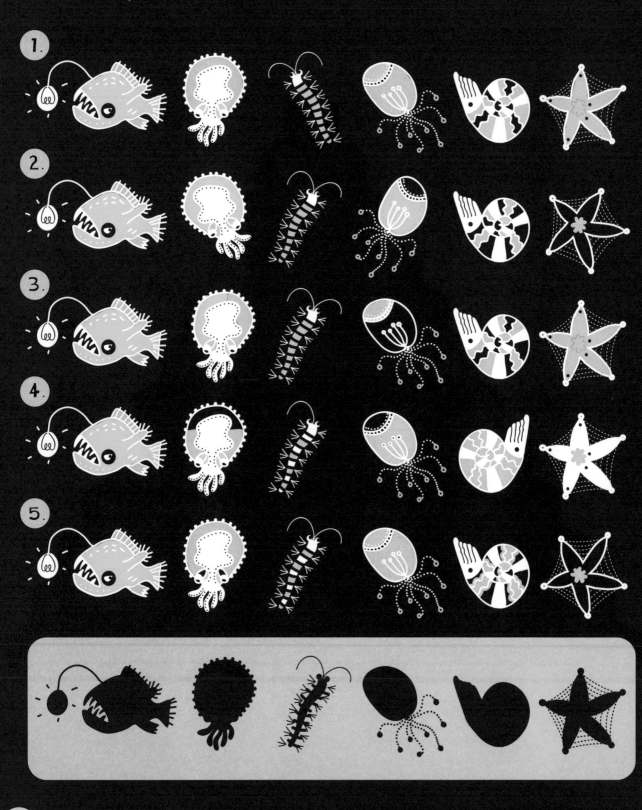

Dinner time! Who's eating what?

Add stripes to the bees so that each row
(across, down, and diagonal) adds up to 15 stripes.

Buzzzzz!

Can you complete this picture grid? Fill in all of the boxes with one of the four pictures. Every column, row, and four-square block must contain one of each.

QUICK QUIZ!

1. Why do elephants have big ears?

    a) To help them fly   b) To keep the sun out of their eyes

    c) To keep them cool   d) To keep their glasses on

2. How old is the world's oldest living tree?

    a) 95 years old   b) 950 years old

    c) 9,550 years old   d) 95,550 years old

3. The largest rainforest on Earth is called?

    a) eBay   b) The Congo   c) The Amazon   d) Agnes

4. The highest mountain peak on Earth is on which of these?

    a) Mount Everest   b) Mountain Big Rock

    c) Mount Etna   d) Mount Ain

5. The biggest pig ever weighed more than 2,500 pounds and was 9 feet long! What was his name?

    a) Giant Geoff   b) Big Bill

    c) Huge Henry   d) Biggus Piggus

Only two of these birds have identical patterns.
Can you spot them?

Which monkey gets back to the baby monkey first?
Work out the sums. The monkey with the highest total wins!
Use a separate piece of paper if you need to.

11 + 3

9 x 8

5 + 7

14 - 9

10 - 3

5 x 9

13 + 3

36 ÷ 6

28 ÷ 7

3 x 5

12 x 3

17 - 8

A

B

Can you find these squares in the picture below?

Can you break this code
to reveal the picture?
Color in each of the squares
in this list to see what is hidden.

A - 10, 11, 12, 13
B - 9, 14
C - 8, 15
D - 3, 4, 5, 6, 7, 11, 15
E - 2, 15
F - 1, 2, 3, 4, 5, 6, 7, 8, 15
G - 9, 13, 14
H - 10, 11, 12
I - 2, 9, 13
J - 2, 8, 13
K - 2, 8, 14

L - 2, 7, 14
M - 2, 6, 9, 15
N - 2, 5, 10, 15
O - 2, 4, 10, 15
P - 2, 3, 4, 5, 6, 7, 8, 9, 10, 15
Q - 2, 3, 15
R - 4, 5, 14
S - 6, 7, 8, 9, 10, 11, 12, 13, 14
T - 8, 11
U - 8, 11
V - 8, 11

Answers

Page 3
COSTA RICA

Page 4
EVEN = 7
ODD = 9
Carly wins!

Page 6

Page 10

```
F Y D I V E R S V M S H H S H K
I S X K T U R T P E U S X T M I T
S S Q S P E C I E S I L U U A R
D T O U W R H M K F D H S R X O
H A L R I Q J H A L G A E T M P
P R F E V D E B L M A X A L J I
L F E F D S L E N H X H W E H C
K I E F X L L L A R O C E M S A
E S R B E G Y X P O C X E V L L
Y H P H S K F M C R T X D H A M
F D S L O W I N K L O U Q W R A
B U B B L E S X D X P V X U K S
Q L G X J F H N X M U K E L P L
G R O C E A N S H E S K L E S M
J A L S E A W R E F L L E H K P
K B A D E E P S E A X M B A R C
```

Page 11

Page 12

Page 13

Page 16

Page 17

Page 15 –
1. True
2. False
3. True
4. False
5. True
6. False
(They take two!)

46

Page 18

Page 20

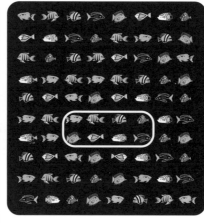

Page 22

Page 26

Page 27

Page 31 – There are more stars.

Pages 28–29

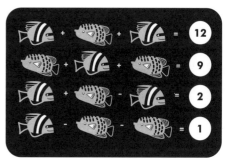

Page 30

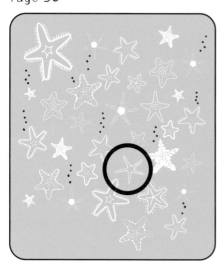

Page 32

Page 33

Page 34

EVEN
There are
14 deer.

Page 35

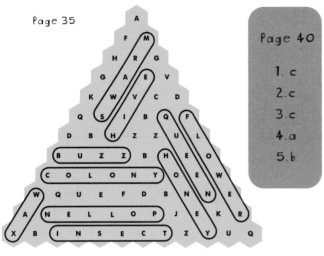

Page 36 - Row 3

Page 37

1. C   2. A   3. B

Page 38

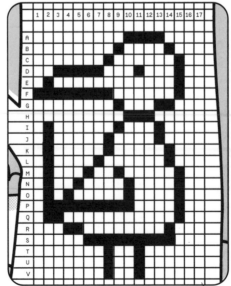

Page 39

Pages 44-45

Page 40

1. c
2. c
3. c
4. a
5. b

Page 41

Page 42

A = 116   B = 125

B reaches the baby first.

Page 43